DEATH MAG

MATTHEW HAIGH

Death Magazine

CROMER

PUBLISHED BY SALT PUBLISHING 2019

4 6 8 10 9 7 5 3

First published in Great Britain in 2019 by
Salt Publishing Ltd
12 Norwich Road, Cromer, Norfolk NR27 0AX United Kingdom

www.saltpublishing.com

Salt Publishing Limited Reg. No. 5293401

A CIP catalogue record for this book is available from the British Library

ISBN 978 1 78463 206 9 (Paperback edition)

Typeset in Sabon by Salt Publishing

Printed and bound in Great Britain by Clays Ltd, Elcograf S.p.A

for mum

Contents

How do we make sense of this ceaseless flow of advertising and publicity, news and entertainment, where presidential campaigns and moon voyages are presented in terms indistinguishable from the launch of a new candy bar or deodorant?

J. G. BALLARD

DEATH MAGAZINE

Death Magazine

6 essential tips for transferring your consciousness to the cloud. Say Goodbye to Skincare – a look at the products you won't be using when you have no skin. *What do cloud bodies eat?* Dealing with the emptiness that replaces hunger. *Pink is the new glass. Glass is the new black. Twiddling your ghost thumbs*: how to occupy your mind in lieu of earthly activities. *New-Wave Worries*: what to think about once money, health and beauty have slipped away with your body. *Co-existing Cougars*: inside the world of yummy mummy duplicates. *Deleting the Other You*: a step-by-step guide. *How to leave a gym-fit corpse. Scare Stories*: what if your keeper pulls the plug? *I Was a Human Fish Tank* – one reader's story. *The Eternity Itch*: preparing for a life without orgasm. *I Have No Mouth and I Must Cream*: in memory of moisturiser. *I Can't Exist Like This*: what to do when

{FEATURES}

DO YOU EVEN LIFT BRO?

No   I slugged out beneath the bar
virgin under stainless steel

We have one final form
& its mouth coughs dirt clods backwards

Lads roll the glue of themselves between
their index fingers like Bishop
when he nicked his thumb

All I see as I heft the weight
is *Alien Resurrection*

Ripley writhing in the muck of
alien intaglio   Nothing

I want to be
could be
achieved through protein

My body ideal
is a bone-white woman
louche among the brood

Treating Depression with H.R. Giger

I treat depression by watching YouTube clips of camel spiders. I watch the mad champagne fizz, black volcanic spill, jaws making jam of a colony of ants. I treat this as evidence that we are in Hell.

And yet there are delicious joys I'm in no rush to leave. Take ASMR, for example. I don't want cars, or millions, or to be a CEO – I've learned the deep soul pleasure gleaned from fingers stroking velvet.

I only wonder: is beauty cold as data? Is beauty *in* data – am I supposed to see beauty in the camel spider?

I dream of camel spiders, I dream of something *other* encroaching on the real.

I treat depression by reading articles on how reality is a simulation. My belief in this is great, especially when drunk. When drunk I love the fake trees glitching in & out of wind. When drunk I'm elevated by the sense it's *all across the beach*.

Try treating depression with lavender. Try treating depression with bath bombs or a peach stone in your mouth. Try cannabis, try walking, try kundalini yoga. Try saying to yourself each morning *I am not afraid*.

I treat depression by running the blades of scissors down my ring finger.

There is a painting by H. R. Giger, in which a creature's coils are kissed to comatose lips. I think this figure is us – socked out cold, the hallucinogen of living fuming through our blood.

I'm keen for the Christians to be proven correct, for them to admit that they have seen this parasite.

My partner said to me *Depression is the devil* –

but what is the devil? – the calliope machinery of a camel spider? – the forceful gas blown through these living pipes? –

I treat depression by soaking up this climate, in which the world's screaming carcass is parsed & picked clean.

Let me keep the perfumed meat, only.

Luxe Ghost

How to detach from concepts of having.
Howz it hangin', Brian? you'd blither to a brain

thunking four rows from the back in its chlorinated tank.
If the body smacks to ground like a hazmat suit

discarded – if the body cracks like an ice cube
in too much cherry cola – does the brain float up, a gold
                                                    ball-bearing,

little shrimp of soul?
How to frame life without eating.
How to frame life without wanting.

Aroused, alone on a dog star, bare feet slapping hardwood.
Feverish with Bvlgari, thick as heaven paste.

We Will Not Become the Cloud, the Cloud Will Become Us

4% .... all clouds converge to form god's face

6% .... I leave myself behind in groups of other men/glass
boy on a stool/ changing room's slick tile

17%...... the tearing of ourselves/ blistered light rhizomes

22%...... life's shit accrues/ sucrose of plums pooling

31%...... the crematoriums are stoked in October/horses
stand flank-deep in alabaster ash

39%...... your lavender skin lives in the nostrils of a horse

51%...... I'd be hanged in some places just for loving him—
sick crowd slouching as dreams leak like rainbow-
crisp piñata shit

70%...... masked men hurling other men from rooftops

86% ..... scoffing sausage rolls in the car park rain

99%...... leaving behind zones of sheer consumption

{FITNESS}

Marlon Brando

Taking on the role of a real
man, Brando played the part
humiliated. He was cruel but
charismatic. Women threw
their hotel room keys at the
perfect American father.
Essentially, sport is sexuality. In
locker rooms the male is a tool
to entice and intimidate. Before
the lean, strong body, there was
the earthquake of effeminate.

Jean Claude Van Damme

Unlike action heroes, Van Damme – a ballet student – could move with the flexibility of fabulous birds, which is why he was initially cast as the Dowager Princess Augusta opposite Arnie in *Predator*. It was a film about the botanical gardens at Kew. In the *Mr Belgium* video games, the character of William Chambers was inspired by fantastic landscapes of 18th-century Britain. A karate black belt, Van Damme employs exotic Chinese objects like those depicted on actual pavilions in his martial arts. His muscles are fanciful with Chinoiserie.

Chris Hemsworth

It looks as defined as, say, a bear.
Bicep-curling thunder makes
men feel unworthy. The ultimate
deity exercises while dying.
Hemsworth's physique was
smithed among heavenly guns, as
big as any triceps. Such films this
god forges by rope and by star
(it makes the actor functional).
Suffice it to say, "bodybuilding
is the core of battle." With that
he blasted off, like mould on
horseshoes.

Tom Hardy

For someone neither
big nor hard, Hardy
is so hardy, and hard
to kill. He does a
convincing impres-
sion of bacteria.
Having shed 15%
of his organs, he is
in a lower weight
category. In order to
encourage the body
to adapt, his trainer
employed a tech-
nique called "20kg
of refrigerated
brains." Hardy can
live weeks without
his head.

Brad Pitt

Despite the black
comedy of self-
improvement, Pitt
ruined it for everyone
– his skin fused with
jewels. He popular-
ised the term *helmet
like a frosted trellis.*
Google *What is that
rainbow of moss
that runs from Pitt's
hip to his crotch?*
He was seen using
a glass carapace in
primary colours, but
he has yet to share
his method.

Christian Bale

Bale has become so milky that simply spending an hour in his presence probably leaves a faint gleam. The actor was determined to incorporate petals, seeds and fruits into his skin. He trained six hours a day, six days a week, for six months to bottle a happier future. Synonymous with physical transformations, Bale developed plant leaves as his body adapted to changes in technology. He reportedly puts a soft little cushion between his face and a thistle. Ironically, *American Psycho* was interpreted as a moisturizer by many reflexologists. The precise nature of his soothing presence is unknown, but the smart guess is that he is like a mountain of white lily.

Robert De Niro

To play a monstrous vermin, De Niro didn't just pull half his body out of the living room but boxed with the boss. He also broke co-star Joe Pesci's numerous legs in one of the sparring scenes. De Niro's jaws were naturally strong. What is perhaps pugilistic, however, is that without a backbone or intelligence, he collapsed right in the middle of her skirts.

Will Smith

Will Smith had already
gone from the Prince of
Snow to popcorn dust,
but this Mishima's Dog
biopic established him as
a father in both senses. For
the gangly actor, blocking
the waterfall was 50 times
harder than prison. Under
the tutelage of a peacock,
Smith trained six hours
a day, boxing, running,
lifting. Within a year, he
believed the world would
end. In a front double bicep
pose, Smith says *The songs
of night can only love you,
but I am a liar*. Well, quite.

Bruce Lee

Posthumously released, Lee's final film is unexpected. The level of violence is a dream. Still the highest grossing stamp collecting movie of all time, it involved sex, dragon crime and economic violence. Hollywood studios had hitherto portrayed Asian men as nine people negatively affecting children. Sure, some studies have revealed a connection between authors and decreased sales, but by keeping young males busy, you keep them insignificant. Lee's legendary one inch parents skipped religiously. He also invented *Grand Theft Auto V*.

Jake Gyllenhaal

Those shots of Gyllenhaal building
the internet, snaked with collective
wounds, hit men like a shitload of
gender-baggage. Having achieved
snarling veins, we ask 'why?' We
believe a sledgehammer is for
everybody, but as men we use it to
breathe. Gyllenhaal had six months
to resemble a suit of armour – he did
this by performing 2,000 cultural
expectations a day. When he mistak-
enly ran eight miles, he not only
flipped – he beat Eminem face-down
to a soundtrack of compassion.

Dolph Lundgren

After winning a scholarship
to give his girlfriend multiple
orgasms, Lundgren was more
attractive on social media.
He was talked out of doing
13 things to the clitoris by
Grace Jones, who studied
chemical engineering. While
moonlighting as a boxer,
the Swede trained six days
a week to build quads of
the gods. His chiselled six
pack body-shamed his 5.8
million followers. Five hours
of boxing is probably not
enough. Work, gym, burn,
burn for guys in suits. This
is what taking control looks
like.

{LIFESTYLE}

Vintage Barbie Chest of Drawers

What I love about videogames with poor graphics is the bitty-ness of them.

I like reality rendered through a diorama, a plywood façade, the dryly domestic reflected in pink plastic.

This is why I preferred playing with Barbie as a boy – her assort-ment of accessories in miniature: PVC handbags, clamshell compacts, sun hats & cycling helmets.

My grandparents thought it meant I would *turn out funny*.

But it's difficult for a 6 year old to articulate how few things are as satisfying as the click of a tiny drawer in a tiny cabinet.

How Adored Is the Pink Authority

You fucking gorgeous pixie. Why
have you let them sit in judgement
of your mind when the mind
can be trained as a cloud can be coaxed
with a chrome spatula.

All this glitter raining down &
the unfurling of flags is not for you.
                                        It's for them.

In dreams my lips find your hip's exquisite
dip & this is how it feels:

sediment falling, unforced, finding its smooth fit.

The bank is gay now, Sainsbury's is gay . . .
We were gay before it was cool, back
when you could expect a good beating.

I adore the sight of you
in a dressing gown, but only
via a mirror (that makes it not gay).

Bank notes rest on us like weird plastic birds.
There's one on your eyelid.

Grace Jones

I needed excellence/ I needed not to squirm naïve as sperm/
something android-esque to hinge my hope on/ I've known
so many men who see no point in living/ the teenage mirror
breathes a pulsatilla jungle/ I needed Grace Jones/ her scalp
segmented glass/ her whole self hewn from marble/ these
figures are luminous pegs to which I hitch my glamour self/ her
cubist gleam allowing me to stiffen my spine/ wearing black as
a shield/ something angular/ like the wing of a jet/ something
that will fall with the consistency of water/ I grew up turned
away from my own skin mirror/ the Romans slept with their
brothers to forge closeness in battle/ the problems came when
this was made identity/ Italian Vogue & Grace Jones a glossy
grim reaper/ for the cover of *Nightclubbing* a violet-blue sheen
accentuates that which made her Other.

Interview with a New Father

How are you finding the new arrival?

Even in the absence of light, life has found this little human being. People tell you that you'll fall in love instantly, but you never understand just how much you're going to love a 15 minute workout.

Did you cry when she was born?

You never understand just how much you're going to lie on the sofa and eat some chocolate. I made myself go upstairs in the absence of light, to my home gym, and smash the ocean floor.

How do you fit in exercise now you're a dad?

I wanted to lie, but better to dive down to the ocean's love. Half the world is in gloomy depths. Even in the absence of a sofa, it made me feel so much love to go to my home gym and smash time. I just burst into tears.

Will you relax your work schedule now you're a dad?

You love this little human being instantly, but you never eat the sofa. In the absence of light, life has found a time. Half the world is people telling you that you'll fall to the ocean floor.

Do you find it hard to switch off?

I just wanted to lie in the depths and eat gloomy chocolate. You can find this little human being skimming time. I made myself go upstairs to my home gym and smash an isopod. Until you're giant,

you'll never understand
just how much absence a
workout is.

*What does fatherhood
mean to you?*

I wanted to work out – it
made me go upstairs to my
ocean floor. Lie on the sofa
and understand: life has

burst into tears. The world
is in me; you feel so much
you fall in light. You never
understand just how much
you're going to love this
giant deep sea isopod.

Simulacrum

The snicking of spades coppers this salty air
as we bury the jelly

a coil of ear   a person seed   a gem
through which life could reflect

No   none of that   This is the end
You and I in clover

a swig of Penderyn
boozy kiss in the boil of June

I don't want this marriage
I don't want my own divorce

My love   hold me   a new world blooms through us
We are nature's end point

We're the barricade for the flesh ghost train
that barrels down the dark of years

Your ears   your heart   I kiss the day we met
Tell them *keep your offspring*

The egg & the womb are in the locked box

{B E A U T Y}

My Rubbery Journey

But either way, no matter where I am, when I'm up, I'm a great soft jelly thing. I can't wait to shamble about, light beamed from within. The first thing I do when I wake up is hate. Let me tell you, I go down to the kitchen and pour myself a big glass of hate. I like knowing where my eyes used to be. I'm on a rubbery journey right now, doing something legless from the start of my day. I stay in my robe to let blotches of diseased, evil grey sink in. I leave a moist trail when I have three different morning drink derivatives. Like everything I like, I love humps of matter, curly hair, pulsing fog . . . it's pretty much my ethos in life. I'm the quintessential thing that could never have been known as human.

Hot Pink

Dear Violet,

I used to think that we had sentience. Nonetheless, I've learned less from watching soft creatures and more from punishing artists. The phrase "immortal" calls to me like a fantastic smell – inadvertently, of course.

The limitless torment simply must be tried. A little hot pink makes just about every skin tone on earth look soulless. I think it absolutely qualifies as suicide.

A citrusy, balmy god looks alarming to some, but works just as well for a black-tie situation.

I suppose makeup is paranoia. A natural colour makes for a blissfully clean machine. Try hiking in makeup. Smooth it on, without a mirror.

Your whole face killed the cool fruit of that earth.

Reptile Your Relationship

1. You may have been grotesque for some time.

2. You may be a glacial crevasse, binge-watching the gloom.

3. You may have found the perfect crocodile but find yourself beyond description.

4. It's impossible to enjoy dinner with a monstrous bird.

5. Perhaps you have felt swollen, but get so massive – a head as large as a child – that you wonder why.

6. You may be mimicking feelings that were established when you were ridges of tufted flesh.

7. Many of the fears and beliefs you emulate are the wings of adulthood.

8. Trust your primary partner.

9. If any of these scenarios applies to you, shrug.

Hysterical Summer

Floral prints will carry you like burnt out circuits.
Whatever is on the agenda, printed mules and crying
just go together. None of us wants to be a machine
trying to escape. We would not tolerate a straw circle
bag or bubble jewellery. Hysterical hibiscus is self-ex-
planatory. Even though yellow is going to happen,
corroded metal is unapologetically feminine.

Sex Dust

This feels so good – accelerating my time sense. I can dream my body with light, I can smash your legs or bury you on a tropical island. I see myself as more of a reflective surface than a seed. I love locust oil. I swipe it on my lips, stain my cheeks with it, and leave it on for hundreds of years. I just ... like snow so much. I always carry it in my bag. I will say my skull is a gleamy sheet of metal. It's pretty and sheer. Your body smells so good, like the air. I'm really into the good stuff all over your heart. Exfoliate with evening primrose – it doesn't do a thing.

Eyeball

Life is automatic, especially for pork. One of the most powerful things I teach is how babies can have better goals. Intuition can be ground beneath their own maggoty interests. My job is to be less porous, in a way that filters out the needs of others. A big part of my job is training my eyeball to multitask. It is, simply, overwhelming.

Passionflower Your Sleep Routine

I don't get nearly enough cockroach. My issue is that all I do is smoke rancid butter and, of course, giggle. I tend to scuttle across the floor until my jaws ache. I'm interested in velvet and rotting orchids. Chalk dust – with its powerful antioxidant activity – is like a choir of creamy darkness. I can't wait to try the endless lines of products, their mix of golden milk and human scalps. I warm a cup of charred wood to avoid feeling hairy, and instead of Youtubeing digestive health into the night, I go thunderous to bed.

A Luxurious Death

After years working as a makeup artist, I decided there had to be a death with a velvety finish.

To be honest, our whole lives are unnecessary. The fabric of life is thick silver, fruitless. The person you love has a 100 percent chance of embarking on a kitchen renovation project. We think of death as the heart of the home.

Be vulnerable, be young. Death happens to everyone; it makes you laugh so hard you snort as your eyes well up with beeswax.

The challenge is a familiar one: breathe new life into a widow with a black pencil. Advice on how to die well? I start with skin butter, followed by nude lip loss.

Top Tips for a Sustainable Wake

1. I always keep a million lights whirling and spinning in my car.

2. When I bring in my groceries – a soundless screaming.

3. I remember endless nights investing in an extra set of forks, a cornucopia of canvas bags.

4. For parties where you might have used funeral bells, opt for a paper horn.

5. Knowledge is one of the worst offenders of memory.

9. Weightlessness is a simple way to smell of rust.

7. Heaven is yellow.

8. Heaven is back in the car.

9. Fall in love, endlessly, with your bag lady.

10. I will carry the ebony edges of the world in a reusable coffee mug.

{WELLNESS}

The Dud

Let's say that the male genitals
parcelled as they are in their web of stippled skin

are brittle bee casements
for which a use   besides the decorative   proves elusive

This urgent bundle is the dud bottle of factory milk
which   though twice removed from processing
                                        somehow weeds its way

back through the body's lacquered plumbing
to its conveyor belt   From here it pushes through

the bubble wrap we call subconscious
emerging like a king from some gaseous funnel

a tiny king cupped in the tongue's velvet   a surprise
but one with slackened posture who's terribly old

whose topiary of plush feathered pomp
hangs about him tacky & foolish as fancy dress

The king is also the stopper in the stomach's bicycle tyre
 &   if unplugged   will release a creased
                                        & disappointed ghost

Memento

when my grandfather dies they let me keep his head
the knock & clatter of grievances dislodged

like antiques   he carried the world's clutter
inside this gristly globe   I shake the head
wait

for thought to pool in the cloud-sphere of either jellied
eye   my magic 8 ball

when the skull's carapace cracks I purse the lips   gum
shut each orifice   to keep his dreams from spooling

& cooling on the carpet   where love scenes
like sepia-clotted holograms congeal

whatever life there was has long since silenced
the brain sloshes & rocks in its liquid of loss

What Will Your Sims Do Now?

Like a good nephew, I save your computer
from the skip's slew of lifelong wreckage,
lug its black lake-weight back to my room
even though the tower is now a humming grave.
Inside still live the pixel kids
you abandoned to a timeless
paradise, still frolicking poolside,
spouting gibberish, clownish, in a summer
that will never end. They know nothing
of the absent god act you've pulled, these tiny
Adams and Eves in cherry-print kaftans.
I feed and clothe and shower them, these strange
skin cells you've shed in your swift exit,
my head haloed by the screen's heaven-
blue, the way yours must have been as you
crafted your craved reflection.
Here is the candy-haired
mohawk girl modelled on your ideal.
I push her around her little kitchen,
fingers lingering on the keys that yours
last touched. Her chip pan has caught fire.
The girl's face bursts open with tears.
Scorched walls. Her kitchen is
ruined. I can't console her.

My Robot (or I Stopped Knowing What to Do with the Android Version of You)

I left you/ my robot/ standing under
the blackcurrant bush in the rain/
the house with the lip-gloss door/
the neighbour's washing hung there/
forgotten or given up on/ I left you like
I leave all things/ propped against the
brick wall going soft around the heart/
the pool table/ its greying wood/ the
bicycle's slack chain/ I do not believe
that you end death/ you died/ became
a palace in the distance of my mind's
eye/ viewed askance/ a sigil sight/ I
now look past your metallic face and
each new rusty flowering/ it appeared
to be a gift at first/ this code of swirl-
ing consciousness/ dusk has me surren-
der to its crush the same way as your
synthesized voice/ a sound that you
can smell/ new-car-leather/ hot salt
wind across the beach/ we've lurked
too long/ this coastal town/ I perfume
my hands with lavender cream/ think
gorgeous/ gorgeous/ knowing it ends/
the touch of all these disparate parts

We Are like the Dreamer Who Dreams and Then Lives Inside the Dream

He tells the psychiatrist about his recurring dream. The one in which he's standing in the street where he lived as a boy on a peaceful summer's day. There's only a moment to notice the diffusing lemonade sky before the monster appears. He was never quite sure whether it was a pig or a wolf or a monkey or a bat, but he sees it now looming out from behind the church at the top of the street, a freakish column of scraggly black fur, leather-wrinkled skin and snout. He starts running, and as he's running he's aware that the pig-wolf-monkey-bat has given chase. You'd expect something so huge to make the ground tremble, but the dream is silent save for the birds and light breezes blowing away clots of cherry blossom. He runs, and as he runs he becomes aware that although terrified, he's experiencing a rush of freedom the likes of which he's never known in waking life. The quiet lanes shagged with foliage and the broad, empty roads lined with glittering car bonnets are all open to him – he could run in any direction. Anywhere he likes, for as far as he wants. He could run to the park and hide in one of the capsized boats they keep for rowing out onto the lake, or run to his grandparents' house (they'd probably still live there, this being a dream) or sprint to his old school and hunker down in one of the chalky classrooms, peeking through the windows as the pig-wolf-monkey-bat's giant head passes by. He thinks of silver balloons lost to cornflower-blue skies, scarlet smoke spewed by the jet planes at airfield displays – the way his hair and hands seemed so much more vivid when he was 19. Something implodes in his chest and the dust lives on in his body for years which then become the seconds it takes for dream logic to resolve itself. He runs, and as he runs he knows for certain that the only way to feel this brutally alive is if something huge really did attack.

Dementia as Video Game Glitch

half of me is in the wall   the shop clerk
with a face like a frozen photocopy
grins an accommodating grin   as if
I keep presenting him with cash   not crisps
I cycle through my dialogue
weigh words as though they mattered
The TV is covered with bugs   I say

I still see the corona   though the star is gone
my family   the one sublime egg I cracked
into this world   how their faces slip deeper
by the day beneath a skein of sleep
wiggle self left   stuck   wiggle self right
stuck

half of me is in the wall   I don't
remember now what I don't remember

Oculus

Knowing it's not real & diving anyway.
This honeycomb's a pixel –

                            still you're tasting it.
Knowing your pain is illusion – a PVC raincoat.

                            Knowing this reality is frosted
                            windshield glass.
The dead go on ahead of us –

                                we'll catch them up
                            the violet path.
Our pieces will be swept to a god's creamy chest –

                          a god who almond-flaked
itself

                          – who snowed itself
profusely.
Crisp packet-picking crow

                    soft gas of rain –
                      these are why
you live
(it's perverse – my love of petrichor – I think of all the
simulated

                    smells I might enjoy).
Knowing that the ego needs obliterating.
Knowing we stand at the prow of this ship –

                  all diamond dust and captain.

{ADVICE}

Q

I want muscle as alluring at twilight as in the haze of
                                              morning.
I feel like a deep sea drone with a personality.
It's cultural – the idea that real men work till they drop.
I inhabit the basement cinema of an unassuming hotel.

A

Lengthen your spine in a bathtub of cream Sienna
                                              marble.
Fascial blading, diving suit – these are the looks of abuse.
We have championed physiques inspired by diving suits.
The next 10 years will be like Tron, but with more cress.

Q

The new ideal is cosmetic rather than functional.
I am metalwork of mirror, lamp and bronze.
Is life empowerment unrealistic? Death is happening.
I am a downloaded copy of my entire life.

A

It may be hard to imagine guilt-free gorging.
You are not OK as you are.
You are a dense black box. You are an ocean of pink eggs.
We consistently encourage men to get a grip.

Q

Unending joy would, in reality, be bewildering.
I am a lavish essay on flora and fauna.
Modern day totems perpetuate unrealistic goals
by shaming men into inadequacy.

A

The body is a crisp technology.
Hack into your physical hard drive and activate those cells.
Crying is your heart carved into a cameo.
All our advice and guidance comes from hostile robots.

Q

I draw a thick, aggressive line through male.
To lose everyone means to become a myth.
The floor is two mirrors, lacquered in burning fat.
The next 10 years will be a toxic fetish.

A

Each world is digital, gold with desire –
filled with sleek men, muscles like pink eggs.
Two bros facing each other reflect unending bronze.
We aim to optimise your body bolt-ons.

Q

I've been sucked inside a 1980s videogame.
Fasting forces the body to look like marble.
Measuring just a few centimetres across,
bubbles of despair develop within the body.

A

Stop trying to be sad all next century.
Squats, bro – chin to win.
Robot chefs supply us with glowing, pink eggs.
They've been sucked inside America, ghostly, unfeeling.

Acknowledgements

Thanks are due to the editors of the following publications in which some of these poems, or versions of them, first appeared: *Pink Plastic House*; *The Rialto*; *Burning House Press*; *Poetry London*; *Magma*; *Fake Poems*; *The Tangerine*; *Everything That Can Happen: Poems About the Future*; and *The Emma Press Anthology of Aunts*. A number of these poems featured in the pamphlet *Black Jam*, published by Broken Sleep Books.

The painting mentioned in *Treating Depression with H.R. Giger* is titled 'O'Bannon's Alien D2.'

In the poem *We Will Not Become the Cloud, the Cloud Will Become Us*, the phrase *'zones of sheer consumption'* originates from Henri Lefebvre in his critique of everyday life.

The questions in *Interview with a New Father* are actual questions taken from an interview with Joe Wicks in the September 2018 issue of *OK!* magazine.

All poems in the {FITNESS} section of the book have been collaged in part from articles found in *Men's Health*.

All poems from the {BEAUTY} section of the book have been collaged in part from blog posts found on the Goop website.

We Are like the Dreamer Who Dreams and Then Lives Inside the Dream is a line of dialogue spoken by David Lynch in *Twin Peaks* (S3 E14).

Immense gratitude to Mark Waldron, Luke Kennard and S. J. Fowler for their incredibly kind words about this book. Thank you to Kirsten and Jon for their support, advice, and many years of collaboration. Thanks also to Alex, who designed the cover image for the book and helped pull the whole concept together. And to Omar, who lives inside every poem.

NEW POETRY FROM SALT

AMIT CHAUDHURI
Sweet Shop (978-1-78463-182-6)

DAVID BRIGGS
Cracked Skull Cinema (978-1-78463-207-6)

MICHAEL BROWN
Where Grown Men Go (978-1-78463-208-3)

PETER DANIELS
My Tin Watermelon (978-1-78463-209-0)

ANDREW MCDONNELL
The Somnambulist Cookbook (978-1-78463-199-4)

ELEANOR REES
The Well at Winter Solstice (978-1-78463-184-0)

TONY WILLIAMS
Hawthorn City (978-1-78463-212-0)

This book has been typeset by
SALT PUBLISHING LIMITED
using Sabon, a font designed by Jan Tschichold
for the D. Stempel AG, Linotype and Monotype Foundries.
It is manufactured using Holmen Book Cream 70gsm,
a Forest Stewardship Council™ certified paper from the
Hallsta Paper Mill in Sweden. It was printed and bound
by Clays Limited in Bungay, Suffolk, Great Britain.

CROMER
GREAT BRITAIN
MMXIX